Killer Whale

Fin Whale

Gray Whale

Bowhead Whale

Narwhal

White Whale

Squid

Right Whale

Whales

Other books you will enjoy:
Dinosaurs by Daniel Cohen
Prehistoric Animals by Daniel Cohen
Sharks by Gilda Berger

Whales

By Gilda Berger
Illustrated by Lisa Bonforte

Doubleday
NEW YORK   LONDON   TORONTO   SYDNEY   AUCKLAND

The editor wishes to thank Jim Antrim, Vice President and General Curator of Sea World in San Diego, California, for his careful review of the manuscript and illustrations.

Book Design by November And Lawrence, Inc.

Art Direction by Diana Klemin

Published by Doubleday, a division of Bantam Doubleday Dell Publishing Group, Inc., 666 Fifth Avenue, New York, New York 10103.

Doubleday and the portrayal of an anchor with a dolphin are trademarks of Doubleday, a division of Bantam Doubleday Dell Publishing Group, Inc.

Library of Congress Cataloging-in-Publication Data

Berger, Gilda.
  Whales.

  Summary: Describes the biological makeup and behavior of some twenty whale species, including killer whales, blue whales, dolphins, and porpoises, and discusses their relationship to man and their threat of extinction.
  1. Whales—Juvenile literature. 2. Dolphins—Juvenile literature.
3. Porpoises—Juvenile literature. 4. Cetacea—Juvenile literature.
[1. Whales. 2. Dolphins. 3. Porpoises. 4. Cetaceans]
I. Bonforte, Lisa, ill. II. Title.
QL737.C4B63 1987   599.5   86-16500
ISBN 0-385-23420-1
ISBN 0-385-23421-X (lib. bdg.)

Text copyright © 1987 by Gilda Berger
Illustrations copyright © 1987 by Lisa Bonforte

Bottlenose Dolphins

Blue Whale

Those Amazing Whales

What animal . . .

    . . . is largest and heaviest of all?

    . . . looks like a fish, but isn't a fish?

    . . . once lived on land, but now lives only in water?

    . . . makes many sounds, but has no vocal cords?

    . . . has a skin that can be one foot thick?

    . . . has a tongue the size of a small room?

    . . . can hold its breath for up to two hours?

The answer is the whale. No animal, living or dead, on land or in the sea, is the size of a great whale. The largest is as long as two railroad cars. The heaviest weighs as much as a herd of twenty-five elephants.

Whales live in all the oceans of the world. Every summer most whales travel, or *migrate,* great distances to feed in cold polar seas. In winter they return to warmer waters to mate and bear their young.

But all whales are not alike. There are almost one hundred different kinds, or *species,* of whales. All belong to a group of animals called *Cetacea* (pronounced see-TAY-she-uh). Dolphins and porpoises are quite similar to whales and belong to the same family.

Cetaceans are mammals, just like dogs and cats, lions and tigers—and human beings. They have lungs and breathe air. Their young are born alive and feed on their mother's milk. Their bodies stay about the same temperature, no matter how cold or warm the water.

Whales have a thick layer of fat, called *blubber,* that helps to keep them warm. They have wide, flat limbs, or *flippers,* for swimming, and no hind limbs. Dorsal fins on the backs of some whales are used for steering and balancing.

Most whales are streamlined, with long heads and short necks. Except for a few hairs around the head and face, they have no fur.

Whale fossils, millions of years old, show that whales once lived on the land. These huge beasts were probably covered with fur and walked on four legs.

Why did whale ancestors leave the land? Perhaps they became too heavy to walk or run on legs. Or maybe they found it easier to get food at the edge of the sea. Then, over many generations, they may have had to go farther and farther into the sea to find enough to eat. Those who were fit for life in the water survived and had offspring like themselves. The others eventually died out.

Sight, which is very important to land animals, is of much less use to whales. Ocean waters are dark and murky. It is often difficult to see more than a few feet ahead. Here sound is the best means of communication.

Prehistoric Whale

Thus, whales depend much more on a good sense of hearing than on good vision.

Today, whales' ears are only two tiny holes in the skin. Yet they can hear underwater sounds from as far as one thousand miles away!

Not only do whales hear sounds, but they also make them. The vast oceans are alive with their squeals, clicks, whistles, moans, and barks. "Here I am" calls seem to keep whales together. "Keep away" sounds seem to warn of danger.

Whales "talk" all the time. And scientists eavesdrop on their conversations. They hear whale messages going out and whale answers coming back. But they're not sure *what* the whales are saying. Nor do they know exactly *how* the whales are making the sounds.

The echoes of their sounds help whales locate objects in the water. If the sound hits an object and echoes back quickly, it is close. If it takes a longer time, it is farther away. This special way of finding objects by reflected sound is called *echolocation*. It lets whales "see" with their ears, just as humans see with their eyes. Using echolocation, whales can know everything from the depth of the water to the size and shape of nearby whales, fish, boats, and other objects.

Sperm Whale

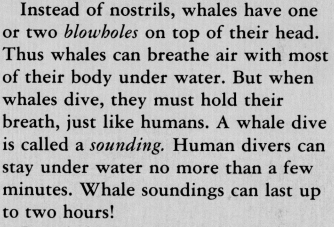

Instead of nostrils, whales have one
or two *blowholes* on top of their head.
Thus whales can breathe air with most
of their body under water. But when
whales dive, they must hold their
breath, just like humans. A whale dive
is called a *sounding.* Human divers can
stay under water no more than a few
minutes. Whale soundings can last up
to two hours!

Do whales have especially large lungs
to hold their breath so long? No. They
just make very good use of their lung
power. When humans breathe deeply
they fill about one fourth of their lungs
with air. Whales, on the other hand, fill
almost all of their lungs.

Also, when whales dive, their hearts
beat more slowly. This helps them
stretch their very limited oxygen
supply.

When a whale comes to the surface,
it exhales the air in its lungs. The *spout*
or *blow* looks like a fountain against the
sky. It can be seen for miles and can be
heard for hundreds of feet. If you
happen to be nearby, it can also be
smelled. Sailors and others have found
that most whales have very bad breath!

Humpback Whales Breaching

The whale could not swim or dive without its powerful tail. The tail consists of two flat, broad pieces, or *flukes.* Beating up and down with its flukes pushes the whale forward. Most whales cruise at speeds of three to five miles an hour. The faster ones can spurt up to thirty-five miles an hour.

Whales are fascinating creatures. That is why people go to see whales in places like Marineland in Florida and Sea World in California. And it is why many others watch for whales from beaches or boats.

One day you may board a special whale-watching boat from a dock along the Atlantic or Pacific coasts. The boat will chug out for a few miles until it reaches a spot where whales have been seen. The captain will stop the motor and everyone will try to spot the whales.

The first one to spot a blow will usually sound the alert: "Whales!" Soon people on every side will be shouting, "Whales! Whales!" If you're lucky, you'll see whales jumping out of the water, twisting around, and then disappearing in deep dives. Or maybe some playful whales will approach your boat.

Whatever happens, you're sure to have an exciting time. There's something new to see on every trip.

The Life of a Whale

The female whale, called a *cow*, carries her baby, called a *calf*, inside her body for about one year before it is born. The cow usually has one calf every two years. The father is called a *bull*.

The calf is born in shallow waters tail first. It may weigh as much as four thousand pounds at birth. At first it rolls in the water like a barrel. But the mother immediately sets it right side up. With other whales as helpers, she pushes it to the surface for its first breath of air.

The newborn calf is hungry and ready to eat. Staying close to its mother, the calf feeds from a nipple tucked inside the cow's skin fold. The nipple sends a squirt of rich milk into the baby's mouth. The calf nurses for a few seconds at a time between quick breaths of air at the surface.

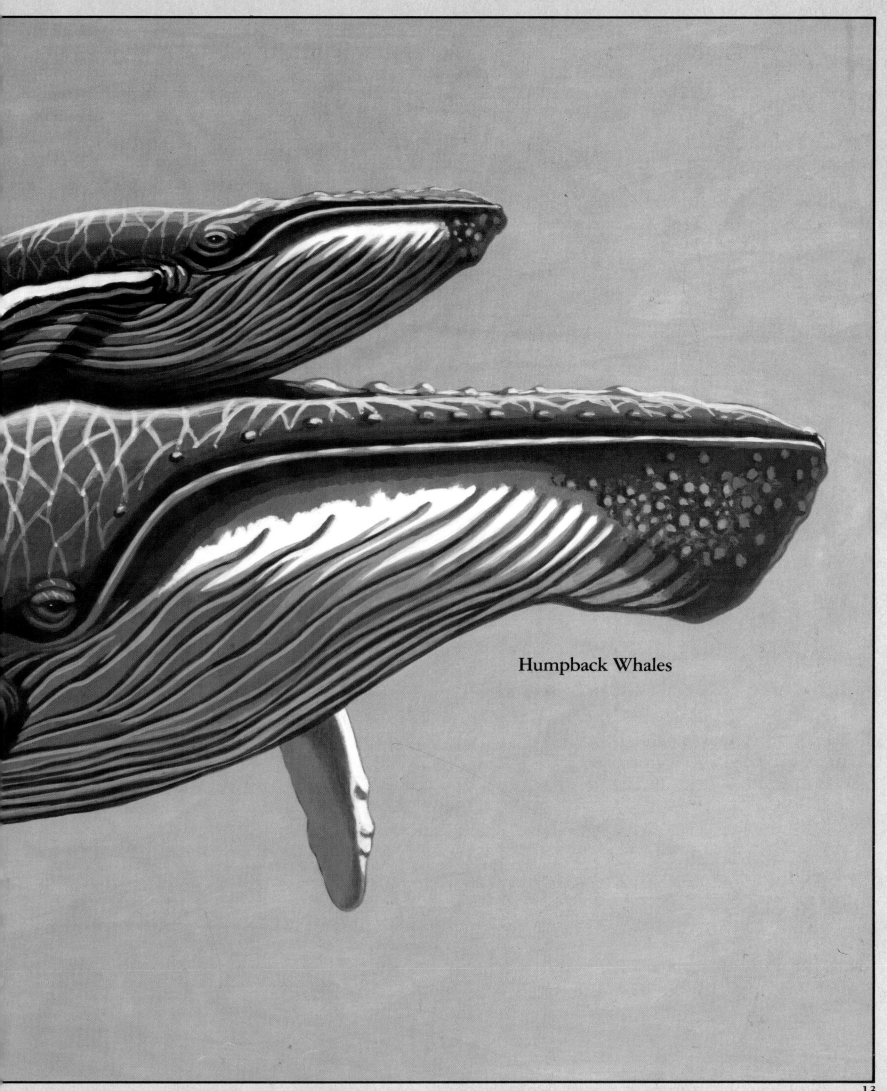

Humpback Whales

The young calf nurses around the clock. It feeds two or three times an hour. Every day it guzzles about one hundred and thirty gallons of milk. And every day it gains about two hundred pounds!

The mother whale stays close to her calf at all times. Sometimes mother and baby seem to play by rubbing against one another. When swimming, the mother protects the calf by keeping a sharp lookout for danger. Calves sometimes swim toward whaleboats, for example. If the mother cannot rescue the calf, she calls for help. "Helper" whales have been known to charge the

boats and keep the men on board busy while the mother leads her threatened offspring to safety.

One of the first things a calf learns is to dive and hold its breath. As it gets older the calf can stay under water longer and longer. The longer and deeper its dive, the higher the spout that follows.

The young whale also practices leaping clear of the water, or *breaching.* No one is sure why whales do these flip-flops in the air. It may be a kind of game. Or it could be its way of making contact with other whales. Some say breaching helps the whale shake loose

Mass Stranding

the tiny lice and barnacles that cling to its skin.

When the calves are a few months old, the whales get ready to leave the mild waters. They need to head for the distant cold seas where food is more plentiful. The calves are now big and strong enough to swim long distances. And they have nice, thick layers of blubber to keep them warm.

The whales move together in groups called *pods.* A pod has from three to hundreds of whales. The trip or *migration* may take several months. Day and night the pod swims slowly through the water, hardly stopping to sleep or eat.

Although the distances are great, the whales stick together. In case of trouble they help each other. Whales have been known to lift a wounded companion with their heads. By holding its blowhole out of the water they have actually saved it from drowning.

From time to time, a whale accidentally swims into a bay or onto a beach. The whale is said to be *stranded.* If the stranded whale cannot find its way back into the sea it will die. Sometimes a stranded whale is followed by many others and the result is a *mass stranding.*

Why do whales sometimes lose their way? Most strandings are thought to be due to sickness or confusion. In mass strandings, one whale may lose direction and get stuck. Hearing its cries, the others come to its aid and become stranded too.

Most whales, however, complete the long journey. They reach the frigid polar regions safely. Even though it is cold, the waters are bubbling with life. The sun shines twenty-four hours a day. The constant sunlight makes the sea plants and animals grow very fast. And the hungry whales find plenty to eat.

The whales remain in the icy waters for three months or so. Every day they take in immense amounts of food. They gain a lot of weight and their blubber gets very thick.

But eventually the water begins to freeze over and huge icebergs start to form. The whales must set out on their long migration back to the warm waters. If they do not leave in time they may get trapped by the ice.

White Whales

Black Right Whale

On their return to the temperate seas, the whales rest a great deal. They eat little or nothing at all. The cows who became pregnant a year earlier give birth to calves.

This is also the time when cows and bulls mate. First they play together, splashing and spattering each other with their enormous flippers and flukes. Then the two whales meet, belly to belly, under the water. Joined together, they leap straight up out of the water, falling back with a loud splash.

If the female whale becomes pregnant she will bear a calf about one year later. Some calves are ready to have whales of their own at the age of five or so. But many larger whales are at least ten years old before they give birth. Most whale species live from fifteen to sixty years.

Sad to say, few whales reach old age. Some die as a result of disease or pollution. Many others are killed by whale hunters.

Black Right Whale

Whales were hunted for their oily blubber for hundreds of years. This oil was used in lamps to provide light. Whalers in small boats threw a spear called a *harpoon* into the animal's side or back. The harpoon was attached to the boat by rope. As the whale struggled to get free it pulled the boat along, often for many miles. But eventually the whale tired. The whalers killed the animal and towed it to a large ship. Here the blubber was peeled off and boiled down into oil.

To catch a large whale today, whalers shoot an explosive harpoon into the animal. The harpoon erupts inside the whale and kills it instantly. The animal is then hauled in and processed on a big factory ship. The meat, bones, and blubber, and just about everything else is cut out and used. Soon nothing but a few scraps remain of the once proud and spirited whale.

Meet the Whales

All whales can be divided into two main families. One group has teeth. Not surprisingly, they are called toothed whales, or *Odontoceti* (pronounced oh-dont-oh-SEE-tee).

The other group has no teeth. Instead they have rows of *baleen* that look like hundreds of giant fingernails hanging down from their upper jaws. They are known as baleen whales, or *Mysticeti* (pronounced mi-sti-SEE-tee).

Of the nearly one hundred kinds of whales, there are far more species of toothed whales than of baleen whales.

The Toothed Whales

Toothed whales have from two to over fifty teeth. The teeth are for catching prey, not chewing. All toothed whales swallow their food whole and alive. Although they feed on many kinds of fish, toothed whales seem to like the soft, octopuslike squid best. The squid may be as small as cucumbers or as large as canoes.

Toothed whales have two other special traits. Each has one blowhole, not two. And most males are larger than the females.

Sei Whale (Baleen Whale)

Sperm Whale (Toothed Whale)

The SPERM WHALE is by far the biggest toothed whale. From ships at sea, the sperm whale looks more like a moving mountain than a mammal. It is also the easiest to recognize. An enormous boxlike head makes up a huge part of its body. Lining its lower jaw are up to fifty of the largest teeth of any living creature. Each tooth is several inches long and weighs a half pound!

The sperm whale dives very deep to reach the squid it loves to eat. Before taking the plunge, the sperm whale jackknifes and lifts its great flat tail out of the water. Down it sinks, like a sleek submarine, more than a half mile under the water. The whale nabs as many squid as possible. Some very large squid fight back with their beak and tentacles. But most lose the battle and are swallowed down in one gulp. After an hour or more the whale comes up for air. The tall, slender spout it lets out reaches as high as a ship's mast.

Sperm whales are very social creatures. They are often seen leaping out of the water side by side.

Numbers of mighty sperm whales roam the oceans in closely knit groups. They keep in touch with high-pitched clicking sounds and low creaky noises. Each whale has its own tune. A harpooned or frightened sperm whale can send warning signals to other whales within a six-mile range.

The sperm whale's head contains a large supply of oil. Whalers once hunted the sperm whale just for this oil. From the skull of each captured bull they got about ten barrels of oil which was then used to make candles and face creams.

Within the animal kingdom, the sperm whale holds many records. It has the largest brain—six times heavier than the human brain. Its skin, which has been measured at fourteen inches, is the thickest of any animal. And its layer of blubber is about one foot deep!

NARWHALS are perhaps the oddest-looking of all whales. Most have two teeth. But in the male, the left tooth is an eight-foot-long, sharp, twisted tusk that juts straight out of its mouth! The exact purpose of the tusk is a mystery. Young narwhals seem to use them for play-fighting. Adult tusks may help to attract females, like deer antlers or peacock tails. Or the tusk may be a tool for digging in the mud on the ocean bottom.

Narwhal

For a long time, the tusk has been sold as the horn of the legendary and magical unicorn. Even today some will buy narwhal tusks, thinking they will bring good luck. A tusk sells for about five thousand dollars.

Narwhals grow up to fifteen feet long (not counting the tusk), and weigh about two tons. Because of their dull gray color, swollen bodies, and habit of swimming belly up, they sometimes look dead. Norwegians took the name of these animals from the word *narhval*, meaning "corpse whale."

Pods of narwhals move together through the deep, icy waters of the Arctic where they live. Many are still hunted by the Eskimos who eat the meat, the four-inch-thick blubber, and the raw skin, which they call *muktuk*. They make tools from the tusk.

A close relative of the narwhal is the BELUGA or WHITE WHALE. The beluga has a very high, rounded forehead, called a *melon,* which is important in sending and receiving sound signals.

Sailors call the beluga the "sea canary" because it sometimes trills like a songbird. But unlike any canary you may know, it also whistles, clicks, growls, and squeals. In Russia, a very loud person is said to "squeal like a beluga."

Belugas swim through the icy seas of the far north in large, noisy pods. Some of the sounds they make are for exchanging information with other belugas. But the clicks seem to be used just for locating food.

Newborns are brownish or gray, but the color fades with age. By five or so the belugas are pure white all over. With their forty or so teeth, they catch many kinds of fish, shrimp, and crabs.

Dolphins are perhaps the best-known of all toothed whales. Although there are about fifty different species, all have birdlike beaks—perfect for plunging into sand and pulling out sea cucumbers—and sharp teeth—perfect for snatching fast-moving fish. According to a new theory, the dolphins send out powerful bursts of sound. The sounds are thought to stun and confuse the prey, making them easy to capture.

Dolphins spend a large part of each day in fun and games. The young enjoy rubbing up against each other and playing underwater tag. The older ones look after the pod.

White Whale With Calf

Dolphin "talk" fascinates humans. Each bark, squeal, squawk, and whistle seems to have a special meaning. One scientist made a record of seven different dolphin sounds. He played them back under water to see what would happen. The third sound brought a dolphin right to his side. The animal had recognized its own whistle. Now the dolphin made the exact same sound again. But this time it added a few more notes. It seemed confused when nobody answered.

Most people find the BOTTLENOSE DOLPHIN particularly lovable. One bottlenose named Flipper was taught to play a starring role in its very own TV show. Others, such as Poko at Sea Life Park in Hawaii, learn to do hundreds of "tricks"—from jumping through hoops to playing basketball. And numbers more train to deliver messages, rescue divers, and carry naval missiles and other heavy loads.

Scientists give the bottlenose dolphin very high marks for intelligence and curiosity. A diver once tossed a metal fish into the water. The dolphin blasted the object with high-pitched sounds. It touched it with its flippers. It even put the fish on the tip of its nose for a very close look. Apparently convinced that it wasn't good enough to eat, the dolphin dropped it and swam away.

When keepers throw food into their tanks, the dolphins emit clicking sounds and swim right to it. Even with blinders on, a bottlenose can find fish and steer clear of danger. If necessary, it will jump clear of the water to avoid swimming into a net.

The COMMON DOLPHIN swims very hard and fast without tiring. Great numbers of them often leap alongside moving ships for long stretches of time or enjoy free rides in the ship's wake. Sometimes they turn on their sides and gaze up at the ship. This gives sailors on deck a good look at their pointed snouts, small teeth, and slender bodies. From close up, they can even see the dark streak from jaw to flipper that gives the common dolphin a Buddha-like smile.

Since the time of the Greeks and Romans, some swimmers have claimed to have been saved by these dolphin. One of the oldest tales is from ancient Greece. It tells of the wealthy poet and musician Arion, who was returning home by ship from Italy when the crew decided to kill him and steal his treasure. Arion asked to sing one last song before being thrown overboard.

The beautiful music attracted a number of dolphins to the side of the ship. After Arion was flung into the sea, the dolphins lifted him with their flippers and carried him safely to shore.

The KILLER WHALE is the biggest dolphin and the meanest-looking whale of all. Its fifty large, curved teeth are fearsome weapons of prey. While it eats mainly fish and squid, a killer whale will attack other whales, penguins, seals, and walruses. Some killers may distract a mother whale, for example, and then go after her baby. One favorite food seems to be the huge

Common Dolphins

Killer Whales

tongue and lips of baleen whales. Although the baleens often form a circle to protect themselves or try to beat off the killers with blows from their tails, they still often fall victim to the hungry giants.

Oddly enough, captured killer whales are usually very gentle. In 1965, a marine biologist named Ted Griffin brought a twenty-foot killer whale, which he named Namu, from the Pacific Coast of Canada to an aquarium in Seattle, Washington. Namu let Ted swim in its tank, ride on its back, and brush its teeth. On exhibit Namu performed like a talented acrobat. Like other killer whales, its favorite act was *spy-hopping* or poking the head out of the water to take a look around.

The beautiful killer whale is found in all the world's oceans. Even from far away, its impressive swordlike fin is easy to see sticking up above the surface when it swims. The huge fin keeps the whale steady in the water as it reaches speeds up to thirty miles an hour.

The killer family travels in closely knit groups. Pods of twenty or more seem to stay intact year after year. When swimming they keep in touch all the time by sliding up against one another. When a mother whale is afraid for her young she moves in close and "speaks" to it. One wounded mother kept circling her calf, in order to protect it as long as she could. Another wandered for three days near the place where her calf was killed.

The FALSE KILLER WHALE is smaller and thinner than the killer whale, and almost all black. When its mouth is open, there is a scary view of its many large white teeth. While it also eats fish and squid, the false killer is not nearly as ferocious as its larger cousin.

False killers roam the warmer oceans of the world in very big groups. Numbers often become stranded on shore. When rescuers coax them out to sea, some swim away. But many others return and get stuck again. The worst mass stranding of false killers occurred on October 10, 1946, when 835 of them died on the beach at Mar del Plata, Argentina.

False killers get used to captivity better than most other whales. One false killer at the Miami Seaquarium was trained to jump nearly twenty feet in the air to catch a fish. Another at Marineland of the Pacific picked up some amazing skills just by watching the trained dolphins.

Most dolphins are found in ocean waters. But a few species, like the GANGES RIVER DOLPHIN, CHINESE RIVER DOLPHIN, and LA PLATA RIVER DOLPHIN, make their homes in freshwater rivers, usually in South America and Asia.

Freshwater dolphins are practically blind. Yet they are able to nuzzle

Freshwater Dolphins

Melon Headed Whale

Harbor Porpoises

creatures out from the mud with their beaks. And they catch bottom-dwelling fish by listening to the echoes of sounds they make.

Even though freshwater dolphins are easy to catch and tasty to eat, they are seldom hunted. Killing them is thought to bring bad luck. And some still mistakenly believe that using candles made of their fat causes blindness.

People often confuse porpoises with dolphins. But they can be told apart by their snouts. The porpoise snout is blunt. It is not formed into a beak like that of the dolphin. Also, porpoises have spade-shaped teeth, while dolphins' teeth are cone-shaped.

The HARBOR PORPOISE is a small, stocky creature that lives in shallow, coastal waters. Because it swims quite close to shore, the harbor porpoise often gets tangled up in fishing nets by accident. But even more, it gets sick and dies as a result of the high levels of pollution along many shores.

Harbor porpoises usually travel in pairs or small groups. People on shore or in small boats often spot them swimming with a slow rolling motion or leaping about playfully. When feeding, they bob up to the surface frequently to breathe. The soft puffing sound they make gives them the odd nickname "puffing pig."

The Baleen Whales

Most of the world's very large whales have baleen in their mouths, not teeth. The baleen acts like a built-in strainer, filtering food out from the seawater that the whales take into their mouths.

Baleen whales occasionally feed on small fish. But mostly they eat a mixture of tiny plants and animals called *plankton.* In the plankton are great numbers of shrimplike creatures called *krill.* Each one is about the size of your little finger. Immense numbers of these little animals form giant red-orange carpets in the upper layers of the polar seas.

As the baleen whale approaches a mass of krill, it opens its gigantic mouth very wide. Tons of water, filled with millions of the small animals, flow right in. The whale then closes its mouth and raises its massive tongue. This forces the water out between the baleen plates. But it leaves the krill trapped on the rough inner edges of the baleen. The whale then swallows its dinner and is ready for the next mouthful.

Baleen whales are generally graceful and peaceful. When chased, they are often easy to catch. All have double blowholes. Among the baleen whales, the females tend to be larger than the males.

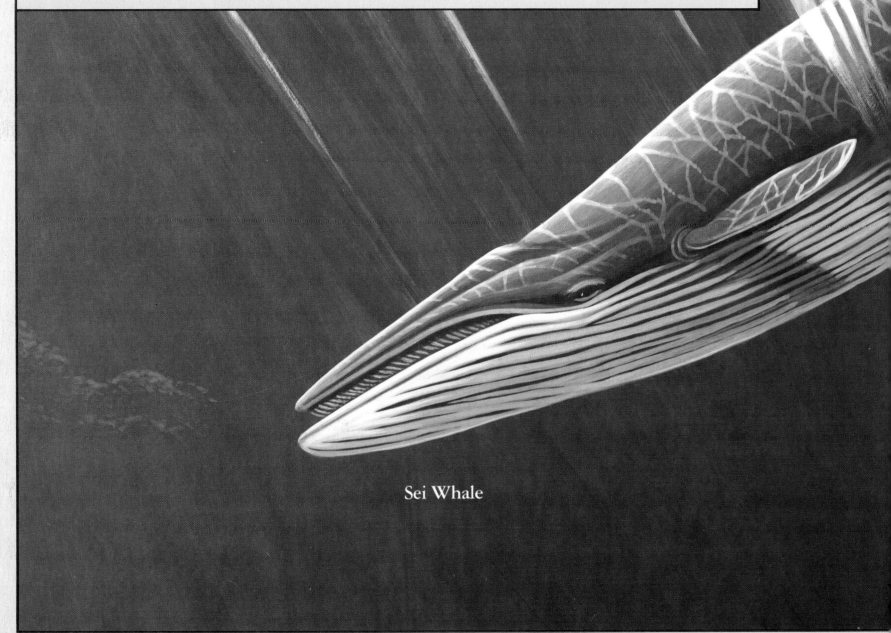

Sei Whale

The biggest of the baleen whales are called *rorquals* (ror-kwels). Rorquals have deep grooves on the underside of the body that extend from the chin to the belly. The grooves are like huge accordion pleats. They spread open when the whale is feeding, making the whale's mouth far larger than usual.

The BLUE WHALE is the most incredible rorqual. No creature, including the mightiest dinosaur, is larger or heavier. Everything about the blue whale is tremendous. It is the length of three buses (one hundred feet), the weight of twenty-five elephants (one hundred and forty tons), and the height of a two-story building (twenty feet)! Its heart is the size of a small automobile. A human could crawl through its main artery. Fifty people could stand on its tongue.

The blue whale also has the most fantastic appetite in the world. When feeding, its expandable mouth fills with seventy tons of water at a time. Its six-thousand-pound tongue squeezes the water out past the baleen plates that line its giant mouth. In one day, the blue gulps down about four tons of krill!

Blues eat day and night during the months when they are in the oceans around the north and south poles. During the rest of the year, when they are migrating or in warmer waters, they hardly eat at all. They mostly live off their twenty tons of blubber.

This giant whale is dark blue, except for some yellow on its underside. The yellow comes from small sea creatures that cling to its belly. This gives the blue the nickname "sulphur bottom."

Blue whales are found in all oceans. Their tall, thick spouts, which may reach up to thirty feet, really stand out. The moaning sounds they make under the water can be heard for hundreds of miles.

Many blues are fast, powerful swimmers. When frightened, they can reach speeds of thirty miles per hour. A harpooned blue once pulled a ninety-foot boat seven hours for a distance of fifty miles. And that with the boat's two engines running at full speed—*in reverse!*

Curiosity kills many young blues. They often swim toward boats that are out to catch them. Also, the blues have been hunted cruelly. In the 1920s, there were about two hundred thousand blues in the Antarctic alone. Today there are only about ten thousand in the whole world.

The FIN WHALE is smaller than the blue but bigger than the sperm whale. Its name comes from the two-foot-tall hooked fin that sticks up from its back. Despite its great bulk—sixty-five feet long, fifty tons—the fin whale looks slender and elegant. One blow from its "flyswatter" flukes could probably crush a grown person.

Fin Whale

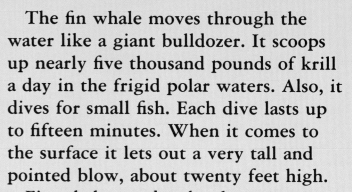

The fin whale moves through the water like a giant bulldozer. It scoops up nearly five thousand pounds of krill a day in the frigid polar waters. Also, it dives for small fish. Each dive lasts up to fifteen minutes. When it comes to the surface it lets out a very tall and pointed blow, about twenty feet high.

Fin whales used to be the most numerous of the rorquals. As many as four hundred thousand fins once roamed the seas. After years of whaling, they are now an endangered species.

Norwegians named the SEI WHALE (pronounced say) after a popular fish that appears off their coasts at the same time of year as the whale. The sei, which lives in all the oceans of the world, may be the fastest-swimming whale. A Japanese scientist once clocked it at an amazing thirty-five miles an hour! Because it twists and turns like a small fish when swimming fast, some call it the sardine whale.

The sei often swims just below the surface of the water, skimming up the krill. Or it dives down, capturing fish in huge gulps of water. No matter what its diet, the sei's especially soft and silky baleen filters everything out— down to the tiniest morsels.

For a long time whalers did not hunt seis because they have less oil than the bigger whales. But as the numbers of large whales fell, more and more seis were killed.

The HUMPBACK WHALE does not have a back that is humped. But it does *hump,* or show its neck and back when it dives. This whale is a natural acrobat that seems to enjoy splashing and playing in the sea. It uses its long, white flippers to roll and turn. Jacques Cousteau, a famous sea scientist, has said that under water the flippers look like ghosts in white sheets.

When leaping, or breaching, the humpback whale falls back into the water with a crash like an exploding firecracker. This may be the humpback's way of loosening the whale lice that are attached to its body. Humpbacks often carry as much as a thousand pounds of whale lice. The lice form large white patches on the humpback's dark, chubby body.

Like most other baleen whales, the humpback loves to travel. It migrates thousands of miles every year. In the polar regions it feeds on krill, as well as on herring, sardine, and other fish. Sometimes the whale swims below its prey and blows bubbles in the water. The fish get caught among the rising bubbles. Then the whale swims up the bubbly column, mouth open, and swallows the trapped fish. Between dives, the humpback lets out a very big blow that spreads at the top like an ice-cream cone.

Humpback Whale

The humpback is noted for its singing. It produces about one thousand different sounds. In 1970 whale scientist Roger Payne made a tape of the whistles, clicks, screams, and groans of the humpback's song. The tape was made into a record that sold very well.

The songs of the humpback whale are heard only in the warm waters where these whales breed and mate. Each group of whales seems to have its own song, which it changes from year to year.

Who are the singers? Why do they sing? Some experts believe that only the males sing, and only when they are wooing cows.

The humpback's songs may have saved the life of a whale dubbed Humphrey. On October 10, 1985, Humphrey got lost and wandered seventy miles up California's Sacramento River. Because most whales need saltwater to survive, scientists tried hard to lure Humphrey back into the Pacific Ocean. At first they tried to scare it away by playing the sounds of killer whales, the humpback's enemy. But this didn't work. So they played a tape of a humpback whale's song. This pleased Humphrey so much that it followed the scientists' boat back to the ocean waters.

The smallest rorqual is the MINKE WHALE (pronounced minky), which was named in the 1860s for a German whale hunter. Although the minke is small for a whale, it is still a large creature—about thirty feet long and weighing about ten tons. But because it is little compared to other whales, it is sometimes called the LESSER RORQUAL.

The minkes are often hard to spot. They travel in small pods through icy polar waters, letting out very low spouts. But groups have been seen playing, jumping, or standing up in the water and looking around. Their white flipper patches sometimes show up under water. If you ever see a photo of a whale resting its head on top of an ice floe, it is probably a minke.

Thanks to their smaller size, minkes have not been killed at the rate of the much larger whales. There are still quite a few in the world's oceans. But the minkes, who seem to like fish more than most baleen whales, sometimes get caught accidentally in fishing nets. While many drown this way, one minke was seen holding its breath for seventeen minutes while being freed.

A few types of baleen whales were named *right* whales because the old whalers found them to be the "right" ones to hunt for several reasons. These whales swim slowly and are easily

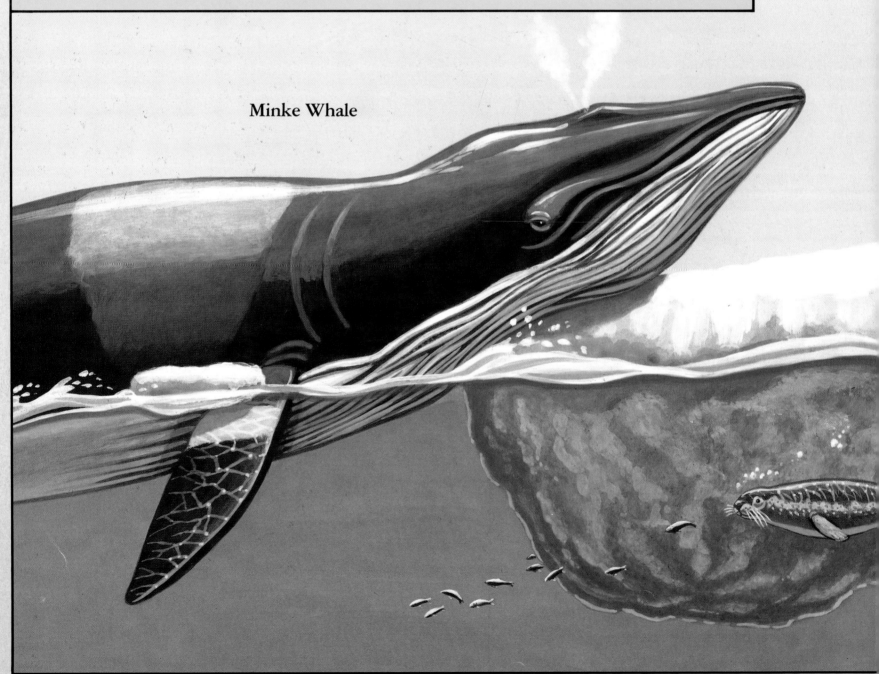

Minke Whale

Black Right Whale

caught. They are not frightened by boats and are often found in shallow water. They have thick layers of oil-producing blubber and hundreds of baleen plates. After being killed, they float, making it easy for whalers to bring them in.

Right whales have been hunted since whaling first began a thousand years ago. Although no longer killed in great numbers, they still remain scarce.

The shiny BLACK RIGHT WHALE, once very abundant, is now rarely seen. The head of this huge whale is crowned with a large, light-colored growth called a *bonnet.* Smaller bumps are found on its chin and snout. The baleen hangs from its enormous upper jaw like a fringed veil. Whalers could easily see its spout, with its two jets shaped like the letter V. Also very easy to spot are the black right's very large flippers.

The black rights seem mischievous and fun-loving. A favorite trick is to raise their flukes in the air like sails, and let the wind push them along. They also like to play with objects in the water. Now and then they are seen poking, bumping, and pushing sea markers and small boats around like children playing with toys.

Bowhead, or Greenland Right Whale

The BOWHEAD, or GREENLAND RIGHT WHALE, has the longest baleen of any whale. Each plate can reach fifteen feet in length. If laid end to end, the separate baleen plates would stretch over a mile.

The bowhead's name comes from its immense mouth, which is bowed, or arched. This whale looks much like the black right whale, but without a bonnet.

Because this uncommon animal always remains in cold Arctic waters, the bowhead also has the thickest coat of blubber—about two feet. Whalers have long hunted bowheads for the seventy to ninety barrels of oil that each one yields. By the end of the nineteenth century, nearly all the bowheads were gone. Today only the Eskimos are allowed to hunt them.

GRAY WHALES have the longest migration of any mammal, about six thousand miles. They leave the Arctic region in January and swim south along the Pacific shoreline to California and Mexico. Because they migrate along the coast and winter in shallow lagoons, the gray whales are easily seen from small boats and from shore. Some whale watchers follow the migration from watchtowers. If the whales lose their way, the whale watchers help them return to sea.

The grays are in a group by themselves. They have throat pleats like rorquals. But they also have slightly turned-up mouths like right whales. These slim whales, which are not actually gray but black, are often marked with white patches of barnacles and whale lice. Whale watchers keep a sharp lookout for their telltale low, bushy spouts.

Grays can become demons when they or their calves are threatened. Old-time whalers used to call them "devil fish" or "hard heads." Frightened grays can swim fast and hard. They have rammed boats with their heads, overturning them or breaking them in two. They have been known to swim under boats and flip them into the air. A few have even slashed whale hunters or attacking sharks with their powerful twelve-foot flukes.

But captured grays are usually quite tame. A gray named Gigi was kept in an aquarium longer than any other great whale. It was eighteen feet long and weighed 4,200 pounds when it arrived at Sea World in San Diego, California, on March 13, 1971. Housed in a million-gallon tank, it was fed over one ton of squid a day. Exactly one year later Gigi was released into the Pacific. By then it had gained nine feet in length and nearly ten thousand pounds in weight!

Many people worry about the future of the magnificent animals we call whales. Millions have been killed by whalers over the years. And even though most nations have ended this practice, Japan, Norway, and Russia still keep up the killing.

Now there is an added threat to the whales' survival—pollution. The dumping of trash, chemical wastes, and nuclear products into coastal waters is shortening the lives of the whale population. Unless we put an end to whaling and to water pollution, the ancient whales may not continue to grace our planet.

Gray Whales

Index

About the Author

Gilda Berger is a well-known children's book author of over twenty titles on science and other subjects. She grew up in New York City where she attended City College and earned her B.S. in Education and her M.S. in Special Education. After many years of teaching and developing reading materials for her classes, Ms. Berger decided to devote herself to writing full-time. She and her husband, Mel, who is also an author, reside in Great Neck, New York.

About the Artist

Lisa Bonforte has been working as an artist since graduating from the Newark School of Fine and Industrial Arts. She has several other children's books to her credit, all of them on wildlife subjects. Lisa lives in New Jersey with her husband, who is also an artist.

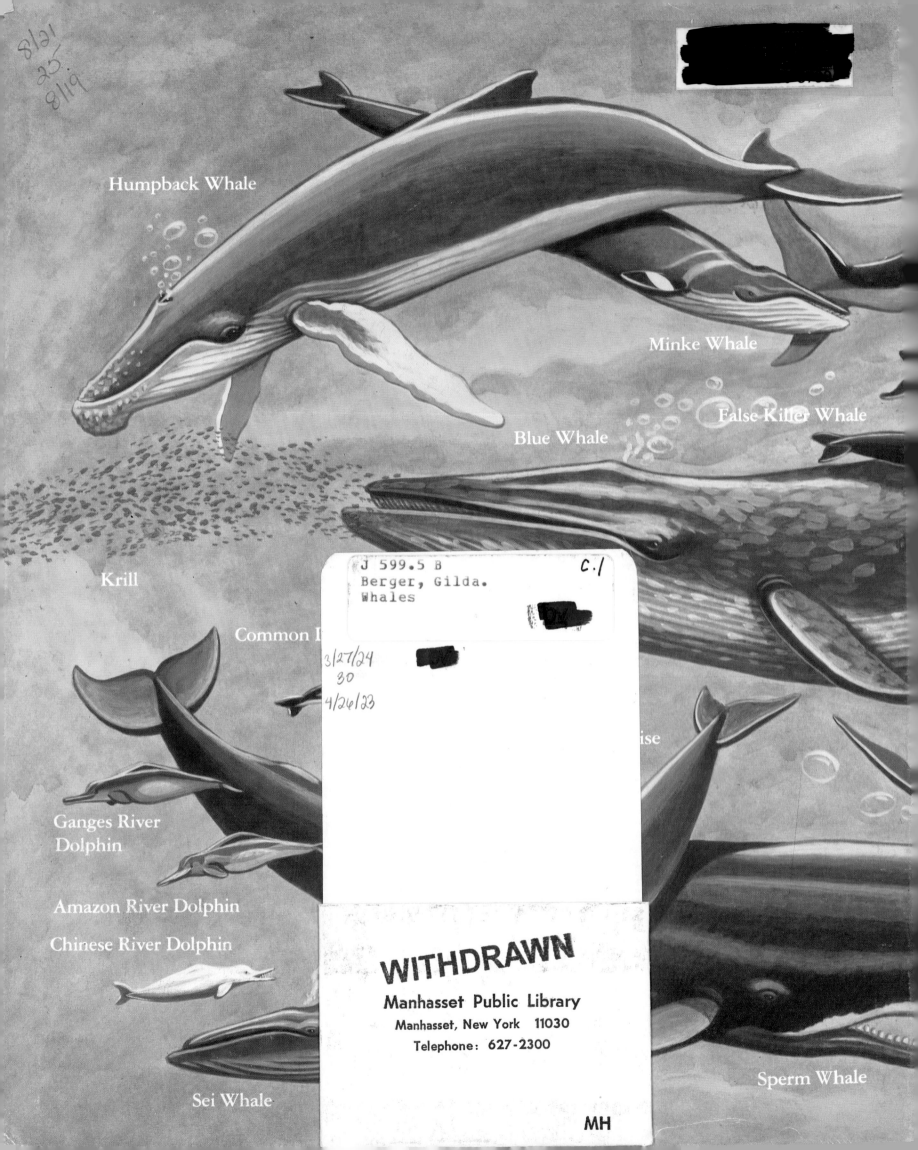

Humpback Whale

Minke Whale

False Killer Whale

Blue Whale

Krill

Common I...

...ise

Ganges River
Dolphin

Amazon River Dolphin

Chinese River Dolphin

Sei Whale

Sperm Whale